BETTER TOGETHER: AN

WOLF PACKS

by Karen Latchana Kenney

Ideas for Parents and Teachers

Pogo Books let children practice reading informational text while introducing them to nonfiction features such as headings, labels, sidebars, maps, and diagrams, as well as a table of contents, glossary, and index.

Carefully leveled text with a strong photo match offers early fluent readers the support they need to succeed.

Before Reading

- "Walk" through the book and point out the various nonfiction features. Ask the student what purpose each feature serves.
- Look at the glossary together. Read and discuss the words.

Read the Book

- Have the child read the book independently.
- Invite him or her to list questions that arise from reading.

After Reading

- Discuss the child's questions. Talk about how he or she might find answers to those questions.
- Prompt the child to think more. Ask: What did you know about wolves before reading this book? What more would you like to learn about them after reading it?

Pogo Books are published by Jump!
5357 Penn Avenue South
Minneapolis, MN 55419
www.jumplibrary.com

Library of Congress Cataloging-in-Publication Data

Names: Kenney, Karen Latchana.
Title: Wolf packs / by Karen Latchana Kenney.
Description: Pogo books edition.
Minneapolis, MN: Jump!, Inc., [2020]
Series: Better together: animal groups
Includes index. | Audience: Age 7-10.
Identifiers: LCCN 2019003940 (print)
LCCN 2019004296 (ebook)
ISBN 9781641288583 (ebook)
ISBN 9781641288576 (hardcover : alk. paper)
Subjects: LCSH: Wolves—Behavior—Juvenile literature.
Social behavior in animals—Juvenile literature.
Classification: LCC QL737.C22 (ebook)
LCC QL737.C22 K464 2020 (print)
DDC 599.77—dc23
LC record available at https://lccn.loc.gov/2019003940

Editor: Jenna Trnka
Designer: Jenna Casura

Photo Credits: Premium Stock Photography GmbH/Alamy, cover; Michael Roeder/iStock, 1; Warren Metcalf/Shutterstock, 3; Josef_Svoboda/Shutterstock, 4; blickwinkel/Alamy, 5; imageBROKER/Alamy, 6-7; age fotostock/Alamy, 8-9; Papilio/Alamy, 10; National Geographic Image Collection/Alamy, 11; NPS Photo/Alamy, 12-13; Film Studio Aves/iStock, 14-15; Michael Weber/imageBROKER/Age Fotostock, 16; Jim Brandenburg/Minden Pictures/Superstock, 17; Christian Heinrich/imageBROKER/Age Fotostock, 18-19, 20-21; Cloudtail_the_Snow_Leopard/iStock, 23.

Printed in the United States of America at Corporate Graphics in North Mankato, Minnesota.

TABLE OF CONTENTS

CHAPTER 1

WOLF TALK

It is almost nighttime. In the mountains, a wolf lifts its **muzzle** and lets out a long, loud howl. Ahh-wooooooo!

The howl is a message. It spreads far. The wolf is calling to its **pack**. The other members lift their muzzles and howl back. This is how wolves find one another.

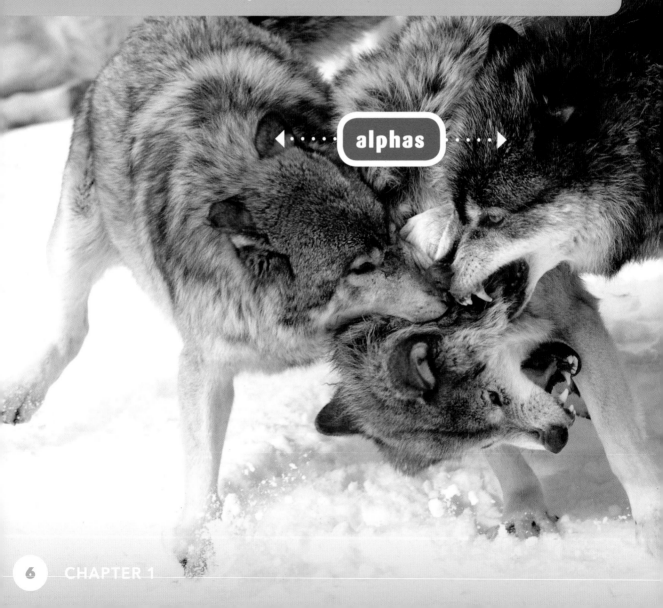

Wolves **communicate** with their bodies, too. **Alphas** are the leaders. They are one male and one female. They stand tall, **snarl**, and fight to show they are the leaders. **Betas** are next in line. They **crouch** low to look small.

alphas

TAKE A LOOK!

Wolves use their tails to send messages, too. Here's what wolves say with their tails.

dominant or in charge (alpha)

subordinate or taking orders (beta)

hunting or about to attack

relaxed

Members of the pack also use smell to communicate. **Glands** in their paws produce a chemical. This leaves a trail of their scent as they walk. They mark areas with urine, too. In these ways, they mark their **territory**. Wolves in the pack know where to hunt. Other packs know to stay away.

DID YOU KNOW?

Wolves can smell scents one mile (1.6 kilometers) or more away! They can smell if other wolves were in their territory. They can even smell if they were males or females.

CHAPTER 2

PACK HUNTING

One wolf is strong. But a pack is stronger. Together, the wolves are a hunting force.

Wolf packs hunt large animals, like bison and sheep. They kill deer and elk, too. The hunt can take days. The pack works as a group. It makes a plan to take down **prey**.

bison

The pack follows a **herd**. The wolves watch the animals. They are patient as they circle the herd. They look for an old or sick animal. This will be the easiest animal to get.

DID YOU KNOW?

Wolves try to scare herds. The pack runs after the animals. This panics the herd. They run. Weak animals get left behind.

The wolves surround the prey. They run and bite it. The alphas eat first. Then the whole pack shares the large meal. It will last them a few days.

DID YOU KNOW?

Wolves are a **keystone species**. They keep animal herds and **habitats** in balance. Without wolves, herds get too big. They eat too many plants. This can harm a habitat.

CHAPTER 3

RAISING PUPS

It is spring. The male alpha guards the **den**. Why?

den

The mother cannot leave her pups. She feeds them milk. She watches them. She waits for other wolves in the pack. They bring her food to eat. Without the pack, the pups and mother would die. The pack keeps them alive.

The pups grow older. They learn and play with the pack. When they are older, they join the hunts. They howl and bark. They are important members of the pack.

ACTIVITIES & TOOLS

TRY THIS!

SNIFF OUT SCENTS

Wolves smell scents from very far away. See how far away you can smell!

What You Need:
- a friend
- cotton balls
- things that have a strong smell, such as cut onion, garlic, orange, white vinegar, lavender oil, or vanilla extract
- blindfold
- tape measure
- paper
- pencil

❶ **Put a blindfold on and stand still.**

❷ **Have your friend soak a cotton ball with a smelly liquid or hold a smelly object.**

❸ **Your friend should start far away from you. Then your friend should slowly start walking toward you.**

❹ **Smell the air and let your friend know when you smell something.**

❺ **Have your friend stop. Then measure how far away you are from each other.**

❻ **Repeat with each scent. Record the distances it took to smell each thing. This tells you your range of smell.**

GLOSSARY

alphas: The male and female leaders of a wolf pack.

betas: The wolves just below the alpha wolves in terms of rank within a pack.

communicate: To share information or feelings through sounds and gestures.

crouch: To bend the legs and lower the body.

den: The home of a wild animal.

glands: Organs in the body that produce or release natural chemicals.

habitats: The places and natural conditions in which animals or plants live.

herd: A large group of animals that lives and moves together.

keystone species: A species of plant or animal that has a major impact on and is essential to the ecosystem in which it belongs.

muzzle: An animal's nose and mouth.

pack: A group of wolves that hunts and lives together.

prey: Animals that are hunted by other animals for food.

pups: Young wolves.

snarl: To growl with bared teeth.

territory: An area of land a group of animals lives in and protects.

INDEX

TO LEARN MORE

Finding more information is as easy as 1, 2, 3.

❶ **Go to www.factsurfer.com**

❷ **Enter "wolfpacks" into the search box.**

❸ **Choose your book to see a list of websites.**

FACT SURFER